JACKO JACOBUS

KWAME DAWES

JACKO JACOBUS

PEEPAL TREE

First published in Great Britain in 1996
Peepal Tree Press Ltd
17 King's Avenue
Leeds LS6 1QS
England

ISBN 1 900715 06 6

ACKNOWLEDGEMENTS

Versions of several of these poems have appeared in the *Mississippi
Review*, *The London Review of Books* and *Obsidian II*.
Thanks to South Carolina Arts Commission for grant support.
Thanks to Robert Gibbs for his now ritualised first eye and support.

CONTENTS

Prelude : Birth Rock

A Way of Seeing   11
Seed   12
Twins   14
Inheritance   16
Spiderman   17
Becky   20
Blessing   22
Messages   23
Emigrant   24
Granite   26
Living Without the Dream   27
Set Aside   31

Part One : Swamp Country

Farmworker   35
Watchman   37
I Shot the Sheriff   39
Swamp   41
Flute   42
Sumter   43
Solomon's   48
In the Wilderness   49
Lynching   50
Pecan Picking   52
Sisters   53
Accent   56
Ambition   58
Love Song   59
Pecan Picking   60
Love Ordained of God   61

Obedience to the Word   63
Pusher   64
Juice   66
Sentinel   67
A Natural   68
Fortitude   69
Rachel   70
Leah   71
Biding his Time   72
Al's Dreamyard   73
Escape   75
Cadillac   76
Southern Romance   77
Forgiveness   78
Springe   79
Ritual   80
A-sea   82
Return   83
Traveller   84

Interlude: Home Melodies

Trickster I   87
Trickster II   89
Trickster III   92
Trickster IV   93

Part Two: Rock Stone

Kingston Harbour   97
Message   99
Embrace   101
Parting Ways   102
How the Wedding Laughed   103
After Consummation   105
Second Month   106

Mother Load	107
Tenants	109
Longing	110
Birthing Room	111
Drizzle	112
Psalm 36	114
Visitation	116
Penniel	118
Cantina	120
Mandrake	122
Lion Heart	125
Barren	126
Meditating	128
Covenant	130
Wash Belly	131
In Memoriam	133
Low Country	135
Groundsman	136
Occupation	138
Shecham	140
Untitled	146
Falter	147
Trickster	148
Faith	150
Blessed	152
In His Presence	154

For
Lorna, Sena, Kekeli and Akua
and for the klan:
Mama the Great, Gwyneth, Kojo, Aba, Adjoa and Kojovi

to Lana, remembering Quentin

PRELUDE

BIRTH ROCK

A WAY OF SEEING

It all comes from this dark dirt,
memory as casual as a labourer.

Remembrances of ancestors
kept in trinkets, tiny remains

that would madden anthropologists
with their namelessness.

No records, just smells of stories
passing through most tenuous links,

trusting in the birthing of seed from seed;
this calabash bowl of great grand

Martha, born a slave's child;
this bundle of socks, unused

thick woollen things for the snow —
he died, Uncle Felix, before the ship

pushed off the Kingston wharf,
nosing for winter, for London.

He never used the socks, just
had them buried with him.

So, sometimes forgetting the panorama
these poems focus like a tunnel,

To a way of seeing time past,
a way of seeing the dead.

SEED

1

Before these poems, there was not much,
just scraps of thought and deep envy

of the giants of colonial verse
forming their twilight words so sweetly.

But the occasion asks for a celebration song,
while the curry and rice still flows,

and soberness hangs by a thread,
as the bass pumps out in the dancehall.

2

Your glory is in what you have not done;
in what you have sometimes treated

as disposable, a mere by-product
of fleeting orgasms, to be washed away,

wiped from fingers and night sheets,
left to dry, or seep into thoughtless soil.

Your glory is in a miracle you may never
comprehend – though bravado is possible,

and metaphors of swords sheathed and
unsheathed, naked for battle, are good

for morale and for action, but this
is all false glory. Instead I can speak

of the ivory temples of your descendants,
the arrows of poison that will pierce

such lofty enemies as would not even
today hire you to clean their shit;

or speak of the tough women who will
stand like sentinels over your promise,

and guard tomorrow with antiphonal song.
Then will they speak of you as if this hovel,

smelling of stale rat refuse and rotting meat,
were some glorious temple of memory.

You, though, when you enter her conch-pink door
tonight, will not know what history

you are making, but that is not your affair.
Yours is to be the stud you are,

grind your seed deep, howl, howl, for all you
are worth, then sleep and perhaps dream of glory.

TWINS

I have never been an expert
at naming artists or identifying slides,

but this image, I am sure, I have seen in peeling
paint, of shapely, carefully voluptuous

bodies, exaggerated muscles, glistening blue
eyes – two brothers, almost in flight,

cloaks of blue and red billowing like the Renaissance,
revealing the curve of thighs and calves,

one straining to clasp the heel of the other.
This birth, with perfect light and cherubims

looking on, is bloodless, wombless. Just this
commingling of myths: the heel, the twins

attached by will, the promise of betrayals to come,
the mess of lost birthrights and the cheating of fathers,

of genocide, the blasting of human guilt, the cross
on the hill amongst the waiting crows – all contained

in this moment, a prophecy of the passion
to come. But, as I said, I can't recall the name –

Botticelli, Gregorio, Raphael, Michelangelo – I sift the art
history books for clues; an unused sketch, a detail perhaps,

but find nothing of this picture's startling verisimilitude,
the way the angels' wings grow with animal conviction

from their backs, nothing dreamed, nothing misty.
So I have constructed this for you to understand

the mortal flesh I saw, this sticky clay
taking me back to a memory of being a brother,

kicking, kicking away, trying so hard
to breath, and fly with my ankles free.

INHERITANCE

As infants they wrestled in earnest,
   heel to head, clutching, clawing;

then tears and wailing until the lungs
   slumped, then they would sleep.

Jacko fled at sixteen with stolen goods;
   Eric the hunter of pea doves and ground doves

chased him with a gleaming machete
   and sincere blood in his eyes.

There was no sense of terrible loss
   as they went their separate ways.

SPIDERMAN

1

Accomplice, the mother
  skins the goat herself,

stews the domesticated meat
  and pushes him to feed

his slack-jawed father,
  eyes sheathed with age.

From the washing she retrieves
  a sweat-stained shirt

rough with twigs and weeds,
  smelling of the broken soil.

Then a raw lie,
  a big unflinching lie he speaks

till blessing comes,
  like a poem, a song.

— Are you my son, the hunter?
  — I am your son, the hunter.

2

He, meantime, journeying across
  the parched land, fingers still stained

with blood, dreams of thick warm broth
  made from the dripping carcass on his back.

He drinks and washes at the well
  and butchers the fresh-caught meat

smelling the sweet warmth of stewed game in lentils,
  so thick, so lumpy with comfort and calm to come.

Inside the shack they trade gifts,
  he gives away his birthright for a ready bowl of stew,

because, standing in the open fields where he is most alive,
  his only birthright is the trees, the long grass, the stars,

and who can take these from him?
  He sucks the broth and laughs with nonchalance.

Spiderman gathers the words of the deed
  and pockets them near his heart,

for he sees a divinity in the anointing of seed,
  in the way a word takes root in season.

3

A stair leads up to light,
  angels sliding up and down the banister.

There are flat stones in the stream
  trickling like silver in the moonlight.

Sweating in this light,
  a wingless angel wrestles the man.

A lattice pattern of light and dark
  speckles these two sweating in the dirt.

Before first light, Jacko Jacobus,
  brain ticking like a con-man, spins his web again,

catching the angel by the hip
  while the others are hauling up the stairs

before the crimson of the east
  turns to dazzling day of forgotten mysteries:

Bless me now, or I will not let go
  of your naked hip. Bless me now!

And in this way he gathers
  more words, pocketing them.

BECKY

These were her words
at the jamb of the door,

her words spurring on
the treachery of their plan

while the old man snored,
waiting to bestow his love —

the angel chewing an hibiscus twig,
waiting for the right time

to gather him up, light like spirit
and take him to his destiny.

Jacko listened with trembling heart
the taste of glory in his mouth, souring:

When I saw your father,
there at the edge of town,

looking like a king in his
fancy suit, smiling like puss,

I saw love. The man had a way
to whistle mento tunes

would make any girlchild
weep with longing. The man

draw me, Jacko, that old broken man
you see in there, with no knowing

of who is coming or who is going,
with his mouth hanging open

and only sometimes a prayer coming out
from that tired, tired soul.

That man was my champion, Jacko,
and I woulda follow him anywheres.

But time pass, bone get old,
eye get dark and mind turn sof ';

and this man forget what prophecy
done come to him so much years ago,

forget that is a generation of king
and priest him seed must give forth;

forget that, and instead him look to
the flesh, the strong arm, the strong back

instead of the soul, the spirit.
When a man is dead to his memory,

then someone must guide his path.
Go inside there and take what is yours,

Jacko Jacobus, father of nations,
go inside there and take what is yours.

BLESSING

My boy, you smell healthy
like a wild goat,

like a black field what jus' done turn,
like earth drinking rain and burping.

Bring dew, saviour, over him head,
bring rain like coin from heaven

and full him crocus bag with pea dove;
ground dove, rabbit, mek blood flow and flow.

And when man eye meet fe him eye,
mek man tek foot an' flee,

or bow with much respec' and understanding,
nuff fear and trembling before dis yout',

for this man must have a strong arm
by God, by blessed God almighty.

Blinded by the white rum,
his tongue loose as a pastor's,

the old man gave his blessing –
the binding words from his lips –

smelling his hunter son's sweat
on Jacko's thieving back.

The boy took the blessing gladly,
wiping the porridge from the old man's mouth,

not saying a muttered word, while Becky whisper,
Tek weh yuh can get, son; tek weh yuh can get.

MESSAGES

Dislodged from the predictability of
anchor and dry dock, messages come

on long journeys; homeless
they echo off the alien hills.

Sweating in a room of raw cement,
sleeping off a day of aimless walking before the sun is up,

Jacko saw a light in the aqua-glass louvers
glinting from the stare of a plump, croaking lizard.

A moth dances, trapped inside the mesh,
no breeze to calm its panic.

The message came in the tense silence,
sending him to places unknown, offering him a warm bed,

a place to plant his seed and watch it grow
and a woman with eyes to keep him honest

and make him dream of love in a loveless world –
this is the message that the gekko spoke.

Untethered from home and steady living,
there is a giddiness that makes the nomad

fertile ground for prophecy;
seed planted there sprouts faith.

Jacko Jacobus travels along the prophesied avenues
to find his true love among the mango groves,

standing there with her soft eyes and tenderness,
just like the gekko said, as it chewed the trembling moth.

EMIGRANT

With nothing but a bag
pack with yam and bread,

a few coins in his pocket
to multiply into food,

Jacko board the ship for Charleston,
with not even a map to tell him where

this black liner heading,
just watching the way it leave a trail,

long and white in the soft waters,
and the way the mountains start to fade,

till nothing else was left but sea.
Jacko and the day grow dark.

Leaving behind love, leaving behind mother,
leaving behind a naked brother, red with anger,

leaving behind a father to bury himself,
a father weeping psalms of regret to God.

Find yuh Uncle Al, my brother,
and marry one of him pretty daughter dem,

den multiply yuhself, son,
till you is nothing but blood and water,

multiply yuhself, son,
so yuh inheritance might breed life.

Jacko meet a young hustler
with glitter in his eyes

talking 'bout how money easy
in the peach fields of North Carolina

and work easy for hardworking man,
and that was his only plan.

Now darting like a kite abandoned
to the wind, trying to forget that him have

a history, trying to forget there is
a place called yard, called house, called home,

when the dark embrace the ship
way out on the Caribbean Sea,

Cut-off, cut-off so far from shore
Jacko toss the Bible overboard,

him hear it touch the water sof'.
The boat trundle on.

GRANITE

His only consolation was the purity of his conscience,
the constancy of his righteousness – the hunter,

duped, but unmoved by the desperation of vengeance;
for in his mind, there is something in humility,

the retiring way of a man, never hungry for gain,
never hungry to make a history of his actions.

Eric mothers his mother with the tenderest love
until her heart is broken with the guilt of her part

in his pathetic loss of all he had deserved by birth.
She compensates with breathless curses and expletives

about the brother, Jacko, the hopelessly disloyal one,
while Eric gently reprimands her for her foul mouth

and her bitterness for the son she loves so dearly.
And in this way, he piles coals upon her head,

and turns her brighter eye to something watery,
dark and distant. He can tell that she loathes him

the more. He determines to stand straight as a bolt
before her failing eyes, forever a reminder of his

constancy, his righteousness. He beats back the twin
of himself that longs to consume his judgment.

Sober, stonefaced, and always there, Eric,
red granite, takes the blast of the wind unmoved.

LIVING WITHOUT THE DREAM

1

For every journeyman traversing the ocean,
    for every windswept con-man

making magic from the weebled stale
    of yellow counter-flour,

rolling dumplings to fill the gut,
    stranded in the valley of

unbelonging, far from home, living by
    wits alone and the tricks of prophecy,

there are thousands who chart their living
    in the predictable earth of home.

They know the path rain clouds take
    before the deluge,

where game wanders unguarded, vulnerable,
    where the wind will blow tomorrow.

They invent the clockwork monotony
    of their safer lives – dreams

are finite as the compass of their islands;
    they forget easily yesterday's pains,

living always for today's new breath –
    death is a promise of rest; the ritual

calm of dying. In this prison of the familiar,
  Eric marks his time, counting his days

before the Pale Rider comes careering
  through the old streets with his gifts.

He has the time to be amazed by the peculiar
  shades of green in this island,

the million textures, the eternity of light
  filtered through the film of green.

Eric does not count colours, he sees trees, nothing else.
  In this absence of miracle, what might

have been is an 'o' level quotation, forgotten
  as quickly as the day of spilled ink

and erasers; the matriculation into the ranks
  of civil servants, so far from prophecy.

On this earth, the simple order of life,
  the known, the patterns of comfort

are all a man needs to face the unpredictable –
  the Kingston roads daily devour the living,

chewing them into mangled mounds of flesh;
  the people gather at the scene, picking their way

through the glass and twisted metal asking, *Him dead, him dead?*
  and Eric walks into his destiny seeing.

There is nothing extraordinary about his path;
  The colony of civil servants tramp

their slanted bodies towards Parade daily,
　　their fingers stained with the mundane

bleeding of their blue-ink selves – they lost their
　　souls so long ago, like victims of flesh-

rotting cancers; they have abandoned the temple
　　of hope. Though Eric, proudly, sports his plastic

breast pocket quiver of fountain pens and pencils,
　　he has no talent for the path to progress,

the genius of corruption that consumes civil servants
　　from Lagos to Lahore, from Columbia to Quito.

He alchemizes from the ruins of his future a way to greet
　　new days with the efficiency of routine;

he steps reliably through the orderliness of his day.
　　It is dark when he wanders home alone.

2

Jacko's letters are elaborate screams of panic.
He scrawls his words in a fine spidery hand.

Eric reads the wailing of his brother
to Becky, cataracted in her veil of tears,

with a drab monotone of indifference.
It is all another country and, besides,

no stone has fallen hard on Jacko, ever
It is the way of the blessed, the manner

of God's will. Eric listens to the lament
of Becky. Soon all he hears is the wind

and then that too is drowned by the silence
of his entrapment – the prison of his despair.

SET ASIDE

Eric builds on dust. There is nothing for him
to construct a nation upon; he stares at the land

set aside for bramble and weeds; this jungle
is a shrine to his loss. He skirts the edges

when searching for game or a bit of wood
to make a fire to boil feathers off birds

caught outside the compass of this riotous
land, set aside for the chosen one, the blessed.

He swings the machete in a carefully mapped arch,
forming an oasis of green to remember it all.

The animals, insects, lizards, all vagabonds
of nature, find sanctuary in the thick bush.

Plant the land, boy, Becky admonishes. *Build*
yuh house on the something ... What is wrong with you?

The boy abandon it, lef it for you. I's yours too.
All in vain. Eric will build upon dust; while

the riot of revolting green stretches
beyond him. He carries his hurt like a man

wears a talisman of destiny from port
to fateful port. Each day he stares across

the acres of land, once his, now lost forever –
the deed signed, sealed, done. He will bury

Becky in its giving fingers, watch her bones
feed the chaos of usurpation. It is hard to see

the pattern of the farm that once stretched
in predictable order before it all fell apart.

PART ONE

SWAMP COUNTRY

FARMWORKER

1

The barracks smell of tart crack,
the floor is a garden of crushed vials.

Glowing blue-black faces suck in the dreams,
their labour burnt up in the acrid mist.

Then numb to the ache in the back,
the fingers, the neck from picking peaches

all day long in the sun, they fumble in copulation
and fall still before completion, naked Eves and Adams.

Amongst his tribe, sitting in the sputtering darkness,
(the generator is on the blink), no heat,

North Carolina's chill rattling the bones
in blasted December on the sweet peach farm,

Jacko counts his pennies, counts his dreams
of better living for his children.

Outside, a girl, slight, sometime pretty,
before her ravaging by crack,

stumbles to a squat and relieves herself,
calling to Jacko, *You got any? Come on over.*

Then shaking herself, she is swallowed
by the avenue of peach trees, forgetting her way back.

My daughter, my daughter, Jacko calls.
The sky is low tonight. Stars glow.

2

Bossman fights the sun with Cutty Sark,
gives out pay-slips, pencilled-in with debts

the workers are supposed to owe. This work
is a hole, so deep it never stops, never;

debts of clothing, needles, thread, a vial or two.
You owe us, says the pusher, smiling,

But in a few weeks, you'll be out this hole,
able to send your bitches home some dough.

Black man's anger, dreams of homicide
restrained, is the saddest thing to watch.

You see it in the eyes, 'cause he knows he is living
for the night to come, for the sweet of smoke

to blank his seeing, that this is all there is,
all there will be. In the drizzle and cold,

they march in droves through the peach trees
picking in a daze, nauseous and dizzy,

overseen by the fat peach-shaped water tank
like a white woman's red tanned ass

with a crack of yellow, shimmering with wet,
holding all that precious water from heaven.

WATCHMAN

The morning he lifted the rusty 303
and pointed it at the frantic fool under the tree,

squeezed a sudden bloom of flame
from his gun, and watched it tame

this unruly stealer of delicately farmed peach
with a black plastic bag and a net,

he knew he had reached a place of sorrow
that he never thought possible.

The thief fell with a loud yell
and rolled in his blood down the grassy hill

into the pond, where the gold fish
prodded at his open mouth.

That morning Jacko stared into the sky
and asked God why he was forgotten.

Cry? Oh, he cried for the groaning man
being dragged off bleeding in the pick-up,

while the bossman patted Jacko on the back.
He wailed to the sky, cursing his luck.

Recalling the careful plotting of his
spider ways, he spun for his path

a bridge of webs, and asked
for light for his eyes.

But as a kingfisher dipped and whistled,
swooping through the bloody thistle,

darting like a moving star
in the half-light of morning,

Jacko counted his blessings,
remembering salvation's path is bitter.

I will sing to the Lord, you see,
for he has been so good to me.

Then he buried the blood in the grass
and resumed his watch on the beaten path.

I SHOT THE SHERIFF

Jacko walks through the trees, the last light of day
pocking his skin, his shirt, his face,

the naked peach trees rustling, arms raised
like supplicants slaughtered in mid-worship.

At the finely manicured home of the bossman,
with American flag and flamingoes too,

Jacko assumes yard posture, eyes flaming
with the last of his carefully stored lambs' breath.

He calls the man out. Calls out like,
Sheriff, I want to see you out here now.

The man, chewing some pork, knows trouble
when he feels it, so comes holstered and grinning.

But the scuffle is quick; no one sees the flash
of machete, the slip of blood on the shoulder

spreading to a blotch in the last light,
and Jacko works quietly, undoing

the money belt, yanking out sixteen
weeks of labour and some change for hardship.

Then walking off, he spits
old phlegm like a stone to the ground.

Bossman, bleeding, points his pistol
but only shatters the top of his peach trees

as they stand, praying witnesses to Jacko,
praying to the coming of a new moon.

2

Morning finds Jacko in Raleigh's
derelict parks, waiting for a vision to take him,

carry him wherever there is some silence,
some hope of honest labour and fair wages.

The leaves, familiar with this despondency
in the park, as old as the shuffling of slaves,

coffled and waiting to be bought or sold,
dance their ritual from memory.

SWAMP

The air smells of thick mud and wild blossoms;
the swamps steam at dawn;

everything is a mist of old South smells,
and the dogs howl in relay along the 76,

where nothing but silence seems to live,
where hunters load their rifles and smoke.

At the Base there is a sudden boom of fighter jets,
then the stillness of the swamps again,

like travelling back in time,
and arriving at a new and muddy origin.

FLUTE

I am standing on a bridge
with wind blowing through me,

sounding like Herbie Mann's flute,
no words, but what sounds

uncurl and ride the ripples
of this artificial lake.

In a brilliant blue space,
I feel flight tickling my fingers

to spread, my toes to splay,
my body to rise above the bridge.

I raise these feather-arms
feeling for the current to lift me.

In this space there is faith;
all is still with miracles.

I wait
I wait.

SUMTER

1

Here an arm plunged into the earth is cooled
by water. The earth is always weeping.

It has lamented the slaughter of centuries,
the blood of discarded Africans,

the grey of confederate dead – the mud
encircling while Sherman marched.

The stench of wisteria collects in the swamp
air, the tears of a generation mist

everything on Southern mornings. It is not wind,
that bows the bearded magnolia down.

I do not hear my name in the wind,
I repeat the whispered names of the dead:

Rutledge, Sumter, Taylor, Blanding,
Pendleton, Bull, Guignard, Bultman –

I do not hear a familiar name,
I am wandering in the fog – calling.

2

You arrive in this slow land where the heat
embraces and clings to the skin,

and find your eyes lingering on a familiar
face – it is as if you have returned

home. The sufferers have the same look
on Kingston's asphalt melting streets;

poverty becomes a cultural pattern,
a gene of familiarity – we is family.

In this land the bones of the dead
are still tender; it is possible to

crush the jaw of a slave, possible to smell
the stench of his last meal in the earth.

You sleep through the night. The God of the church
speaks in your language. You say, *Amen, and Amen*.

3

Jacko arrives at the stripping prefab shed
on the outskirts of Sumter. It is dark.

The Greyhound bus continues into the night,
searching for Georgia, Alabama in the dark.

The trees creep inward on the narrow road;
Jacko listens to the rural of it all.

Somewhere on West Liberty he sees a red light,
finds shelter in a club. The rum is old, potent,

tickles life back into his broken self.
A woman points him to the comfort of Solomon's

old-style food – they all know the mothering
of that sweet-water oasis on the other side of the tracks.

This side of the old city
once strutted in two-tone shoes

and Sunday-proud suits and hats,
and women, glamorous as pride,

tapped umbrellas waiting for RTA to bus them,
reserved seats and clean floors, home.

This side of the old city
had its own ice cream parlour,

and midwives did a brisk trade
starched white and regal,

like old village mothers
with their satchels of ancient beads.

At night, the juke joints
hopped to Jersey Jazz,

and stars with slick bright hair
smoked cigarettes with the local boys

hung out on the corner
eyeing the college girls going by,

the hoots getting louder
for the red-bone ones.

Here the beginning of so many stories;
the making of the black middle class.

Now trucks leak used diesel,
and truckers crap in the sand

on this side of the old city,
this dust bowl, where there was once magic,

the heart of our American dreaming,
the pastime of Negro baseball, bold, sassy, brash,

so fast like the lindy-jumping
zoot-suit youths of the dance halls.

Now those were glory days when
in our way we thought we had

the whole of our own pie,
and the road was always clear,

'cause those were roads that only we took,
and our bridges to the rich beyond

were not clotted by other sojourners;
just us with our own compasses and rest stops.

No one talked of crossing no line,
smudging no line, just toe the damned thing

while making your own blues-easy path
to a brighter beautiful morning.

5

Just off the beaten path – Solomon's backyard –
Jacko finds the streets strewn with trash;

he is calm in this familiar decay. Home fires
beckon. In the unlit street he can see

the sharp burst of light like fireflies
and the lazy sway of headlights dragging

their beam through the hedges, the trees,
the walls. As he nears the house, he can see

the faces, sweat-slick, looking like they
think they look happy, touched, smiling –

they move with slow precision into the street
past him. In Solomon's home fires burn.

The earth weeps always. Like an old memory
the flood of sorrow, salt sorrow

is constantly near the topsoil. Jacko
feels the muddy clutch of the earth. It holds him.

SOLOMON'S

But Solomon's still stands bright as hope,
tenacious watering hole where fish

is so sweetly battered and fried,
greens are soft and bold, and sweet, sweet

potatoes, sweat their candy orange under
cheap fluorescent. Solomon's

is the lunch retreat of the city black folk
looking for home on this side of the tracks —

what they done abandoned so long ago
with their degrees and fancy cars —

yes lawyers, council men, business folk,
reverends, undertakers and teaching types,

parking their spanking, bright-coloured cars
in the makeshift lot, and eating, eating

the grease and crisp-fried pork skin,
trying to devour Africa back into their blood.

Solomon's is where the sisters watch
the crazy white folks construct their myths

in melodrama on the color teevee,
whose ironic eye gazes back at this

fevered search for home and grandmother
in the richness of good soul food.

IN THE WILDERNESS

Sumter too is the home of his Uncle Al,
pusher of dreams in white dust

and rocks of diabolic flight
that wait to flare the brittle brains

of the vulnerable. Jacko can feel
the dryness of his soul, can feel

the way the heat teases – he knows
the sweetness of the burn,

the incendiary light in the skin,
catching his breath, flight

and the dusty numbness afterwards.
He trembles at the thought,

turning his face from the tempting
path down into the belly of Al's domain

with its untended yard of broken vials,
ash, and scattered memories.

Jacko is untethered from family and past,
making a new living alone.

Old things are passed away.
The invisible man reinvents himself.

LYNCHING

1

When he peers into her eyes, searching for sounds
  in the startle of her bland face,

she covers her reddening throat and stammers,
  but no words; all he reads in her lips is ooooo.

She leaves the lab to let him clean she says,
  but sprints through the darkening courtyard,

searching for the familiar eyes and skin
  of security, her heart pounding, pounding.

He sweeps to his own distant music
  in the cloud of silence about his head.

2

Without words they fire him – send him home
  for his own good – a failed project.

They read lust.in his bowed head;
  misread his avoidance of her

eyes to be a leering
  at her holy breasts.

He had never thought to taste
  the bloodless white of her skin,

never thought to touch the twitching
  of her trembling cheek, never.

Walking blankly homeward he is still
  blind to the quiet of this lynching.

PECAN PICKING

Jacko sweeps the falling leaves
    on chill winter mornings, denim blue

in the gathering mist, against the steel-grey sky
    with jets booming over the south lands.

He feels the shudder of barrier-breaking
    sound, stares at the trail of white,

then picks pecans from the bramble and twigs
    in this silence, still as death, still as morning.

SISTERS

Her body is no longer tender, but her mind is free.
Rita Dove, *"Obedience"*

1

Glenda is the pretty New York girl
who came South with a dapper preacher boy

twenty years ago. Says the South's
growing on her slow like everything else.

Glenda beats out little bright boys
with fingers that make clever music

on the piano. Through this she earns
a pittance which helps ends meet.

Though a grandmother, she looks ripe
to be spoiled by the eyes of some manchild

who can't see that she's seen so much,
been through so much, heard so much

that it ought to have spoilt her
for being game for courting,

despite her all-fashionable and bright new self,
like new pennies, falling to the floor like light.

Glenda camouflages the spreading
of her hips in knit sweaters

and smiles bright to distract the wandering eyes
straying down where she doesn't want them to be.

Still, she's laughing more than ever these days,
though she shouldn't with her husband in the white man's jail.

But if you happen by her custom-
built home after midnight, you can hear

her delicate falsetto, swapping lines
with Marvin Gaye, rocking a memory,

singing, *Let's get it on*, across the old night,
over the Wateree, across the old swamp lands,

Let's get it on, across the railroad tracks,
around the sturdy live oak trunks,

Let's get it on, in the muggy musk
of small share-cropping towns,

all the way to her beloved,
locked up and dreaming in his prison cell,

counting the years since his sudden fall
from pastor to con, to long timer like that.

2

The sisters meet for fish in Solomon's
each day, to commiserate the slim pickings:

most all the fish have left the rivers now,
and the few left swimming just ain't pretty,

not worth the clothes they got on,
not worth the air they breathing,

though they sitting so cocksure like that,
so certain of their scrawny-arsed selves.

They share their crushes and plans of action,
vowing never to fight over none of these mens,

too tired for that shit, too damned old for that, they laugh
and sip tea and talk of orgasms and how long it's been.

3

Early, before dawn light disturbs the mist
   sheathing the pecan park with its skeletal

trees, curling and uncurling budded fingers,
   Glenda stops for coffee and consolation

with Sandra, the sweet sister whose mercy
   is forever. Jacko sits in his old corner

watching this ritual of love, the two women
   in red and black sweats and neon sneakers,

stomping their feet from the cold and
   smoking cigarette after cigarette –

prison contraband that Glenda gets from her husband,
   Ephraim, who does good business in the joint.

Jacko sees this and feels the fullness of something,
   the way his stomach turns at seeing her smoking there.

Tears come to his eyes watching
   these two women growing softly round.

ACCENT

When she heard his voice
calling for the crisp-fried fish,

softly using his spread fingers
to make the shape and texture and taste

of the batter-thick fish
swimming in a river of hot sauce;

her heart travelled away from the swamp
to an old memory of a Kingston man

just landed in gritty New York,
strumming his guitar in the subway caves

to make ends meet and find his dream;
his coiled hair modestly tucked

in a blazing tam of greens, yellows and reds.
She had stopped to listen,

seen deep into the ocean of his eyes,
been carried along by his sea-water memories

from the grime of the subway to other shores,
the undulation of his voice like making love.

She understood the passion of music
like never before that day.

Now here in Solomon's, so far from the Bronx,
while toying with cold collard greens,

she heard the sea-roll of his voice
waiting to carry her away again,

this time so close, so hungry,
his eyes finding her and devouring

everything in her coquette smile,
her affected way with the greens.

That day Glenda spoke to Jacko,
ordered more fish while he carved the white

flesh in its crisp gold bed
and chewed and laughed at her curious stare,

and after he was full and giddy with
this new old way of finding pleasure,

they stepped like lovers into the bright light
floating on the lilt of his island voice.

It was like light rushing
through her tender veins – purest light.

AMBITION

— And what would you like to be,
when it is all over and you are ready

to face the new day of the risen dead,
and the long sleep before the trumpet call?

— A father, simply a prolific father,
scatterer of multiple seedlings.

A farmer is what I am, born
not to gather, nor to hunt,

but to plant seed and watch
them grow, blooming flowers, ripening fruit,

leaves, life. I plant seed in soil
I have tilled and this is all there is for me.

I plant words, I plant dreams, I plant
lies, I plant my love in fertile ground.

Sandra called him ambitionless, but fine.
Glenda called him a sweet plower of soil

and declared her soil ripe for plowing,
and for planting – she tilled and watered it daily.

LOVE SONG

They play word games in the twilight,
and at night dance to the sound of the radio,

playing oldies but such goodies,
their bodies pressed hard, trying to suck

everything living, everything moving
into their broken hearts and souls.

Come dark, when the labour of sweeping falling leaves
weighs him down, Jacko finds her soft hand

caressing life into his bones again,
and if this is not love, then it is enough,

in this place of clean paths,
this place of predictable cages.

PECAN PICKING 2

Since the news of his father's death,
silence has gathered around Jacko's head.

He thinks only of the shame
of his impersonation, thinks only

of the price of glory, of regeneration in the spoken
prophecy of God – this unclean path to eternity;

not even able to say a calm farewell to his progenitor.
He sits among the pecan leaves and laments his glory.

LOVE ORDAINED OF GOD

At the news of his love for Glenda,
the New York divorcée piano teacher,

with an ex in jail preaching heaven
to his fellow inmates and trading fags,

Becky sees the death of her dream,
the drying up of prophecy in the thighs

of what she calls a glitter-eyed
opportunistic whore – she uses that word

and more. So, gathering all her strength,
she writes a letter of stringent decree

to Jacko, love-struck and giddy in Glenda's arms,
a letter demanding he abandon that path

and find a Jamaican girl, a trustworthy girl
whose hips had not been sullied by sin,

whose lips had tasted only the choicest meats,
whose love would be constant as new mornings,

whose soul would take to the Jamaican earth
without word of complaint or regret.

Her letter, posted with express haste,
startled Jacko from his dream,

reminding him of his compact with the Lord,
the compact of deceit for the birth of a new nation,

his compact with his mother, the promise to follow
her guiding finger as he had the day

his father bestowed the promise of fruitful seed
on his false head. The memory startles Jacko

Jacobus back to the path before him,
and making love to Glenda that night,

he weeps so profusely and so completely
that his prick gives up on him and falls flaccid

on the sweat-wet sheets of their loving.
Without words, she knows his slow drag

of foot through the door into the waiting
yellow of dawn, will be his last.

She understands the prophecy of his unwilling seed,
for despite her prayers and constant potions

nothing has taken in her waiting womb,
nothing of his took root and grew.

OBEDIENCE TO THE WORD

Jacko Jacobus journeys across the desert
of his shame and hurt, to find at a well

the daughter of his Uncle Al. There,
love ordained of God would sprout and flourish

among the green and white dogwood light,
in the squalor of the South Side where Al is king.

And what a wondrous welcome it is:
slaughtered pigs and barbecued flesh,

malt liquor like a river to drown all tears,
and the juke joint hopping, while Jacko droops

like a lamb to the slaughter, his seed proferred, his body
to be bound to years of hard labour for his board

and wife; issuing rocks of miracle crack
and crushed leaves of purest lambs' breath.

Leah and Rachel, the daughters, watch from the edges,
both lusting for the promise of his progeny.

PUSHER

Angelus of mercy,
Al was the Pope

walking through the squalor
of an unfeeling world.

Yes, sometimes, numbed by his stuff,
he floated among the giddy children,

bestowing vials of mercy for the pain.
At first it was not the money,

just the urge to stir the darkness
of these defeated descendants of slaves

to something more volatile,
something like the bepop madness

of Miles, Coltrane, or the crazy
dreamings of Monk the magician,

something that would make
the bossman sleep uneasy at night,

with gun loaded beneath his pillow,
his daughters strapped to their beds

for fear they might catch wind
of this jazz in the air

and go low riding
near the barracks.

It was this at first,
this way to liven the drabness

of nothing lives,
this merciful act

that got him in the business.
But missionary work don't pay the bills,

and what with babies coming from his balls,
and the pittance from the bossman

not making ends meet; and the thugs
in New York looking for expansion

into the slumbering South,
Al, the pope of Hog Town,

opened his missal and bestowed
his indulgences for a price,

while the jazz grew slow and mute
and the brothers floated through their dreams,

not touching earth, not touching nothing
on their path through the trees.

And Al prospered
before the Lord.

JUICE

Rachel stands stone-eyed guardian,
heartless shepherdess of the business

that drifts in and out of the gloomy
insides of the abandoned shack –

the temple of dreams littered with the glitter
of vials and the stale sweet of smoke.

Jacko is weary from too much travelling.
His heart lurches as if it is love for family

he feels, but his better part opts for tears,
beckoning her softer eye, her tender hand:

– *What you tripping on, man?*
– *Yuh, baby, yuh is my juice today.*

The laughter gathers around them
like the gauze of healing and comfort.

SENTINEL

Jacko surveys the crowd at the gate,
and no man dare touch the sisters.

Al has dreams for these his off-spring;
willing them to float above the predictable

path of these South Side girls
who litter the apron of his dreamyard,

sniffing out a piece of heaven
with their babies staring mutely

into the absence of hope. No man
dare come close to Rachel or Leah

with Jacko, the eunuch, standing guard.
They tease him, toy with his head,

but his is a will of stone.
He stands among the live oak trees

in Swan Lake, and releases the pent up
turmoil of his body in quick spurts;

then healed, freed of his madness,
he returns to the ritual of selling

magic in tiny vials to the gullible
who enter his world like bloated flies.

A NATURAL

Jacko knows the stench of hunger,
the reek of a soul in search of hope.

It is a desperate odour that carries
over water; he sniffs it out like a beast.

Al calls it a gift from God, the way
Jacko can read the eyes of the hungry,

spot the limp-willed denizens from afar
and chart their succumbing to the light

of his bag full of tricks. Jacko lingers
on the edges of parks, waiting for the next

lamentable soul to come quietly
into the promise of his gifts.

He has, of late, found tree-shaded spots
outside Mental Health, DHEC, the Oxford House,

Tuomey Regional, the Court House, Funeral Homes,
where the zombied desperate are stunned by the sun

and the bitter news of illness and deprivation.
Jacko ferries them to Al's dream yard

where they take their flight into the embrace
of thin films of cloud, cocooning their pain

like the fingers of a web. Jacko
counts his pennies daily, and the days slip by.

FORTITUDE

Rachel dreams of Jacko's tears,
the way he weeps at the movies,

the way he does not look into her eyes
like one afraid to fall into too deep water.

She contrives excuses to touch him,
while Al, the Pope, is offering the sacraments

to some wayward pilgrim in his dreamyard.
For months, Jacko will not see her,

will not take from her delicate fingers
the purest powder of dreaming she can find.

He is clean as a priest, sniffs nothing,
drinks nothing, smokes nothing,

for this manchild knows the treachery
of the flesh – he will not be tricked by a trick.

RACHEL

There is mothering in her eyes,
in the shape of her unseeded stomach,

in the sturdy flesh of her hips,
in the way her body smells of comfort,

in the manner of a fertile ewe
with which she moves about the house,

chewing with the patience of a mother
the food she magics into being.

She was named by a keeper of livestock:
in those days, Al saw domesticated patterns

in all human flesh – cattle, goats, sheep.
He has trained her well to grow

into her name. Jacko wants to shepherd
her into his pasture, black ram tupping Al's ewe.

LEAH

You could tell by the tegareg of her walk,
a kind of slack, bone-loose sashay,

and the unruly gallop of her uncaged
breasts, that she is staring hard,

a cow with a bull's disposition,
waiting to bolt madly into the open field.

Leah saturates the lining of her dreams
with Al's magic dust – she never slumbers

to dreaminess when she is taken
by the chemistry in her blood.

She leaps and cavorts for days
till the red has left her eyes.

The house is cleaned spotlessly,
the labours of the yard are always done,

and she bounds with a strange gaze
from task to task, her skin dry as dirt.

Jacko can see Al's anxiety at the wild
teated creature; he can tell there is fear.

Jacko searches for her missing self,
but he cannot find her softer parts.

Still, he can tell by the way she stares
that she has the capacity to devour him.

BIDING TIME

Obedient to a fault,
spider man Jacko bides his time –

he has the patience of a stone,
when he rolls over she will see

his tenderest parts,
and then Rachel will wail his name

through the good night. Jacko
bides his time, tormenting himself

with the promise of her lashes
like fingers brushing the softness

of his cheek. Jacko bides his time,
ferrying the business to Al's dreamyard.

AL'S DREAMYARD

Stumbling over soft bodies and loose cloth
in Al's dream yard – Ah, Christmas wind blows!

Nothing moves, just white light and then dim
and the hiss of frying crack – Ah Christmas wind!

Headlights spot the black beyond in quick darts
as midnight sojourners climb the bridge of the I95.

Stoned to a dumb horny uselessness, they sit
talking trash until the shit is ash.

Rachel wants to lie in the grass.
Jacko feeds her toasted pecans.

Tasting the arsenic of the red flesh
she spits and feels to relieve herself.

Leah giggles. Jacko is blind. Reaches across.
Touches darkness, soft darkness. Feels a cool sweaty

neck, then a trail of beads down to mud forever,
while Rachel retches against a live oak tree.

They couple quickly like a dream,
Leah patting his clumsy back like a baby.

Rachel's sobs carry like breathing,
then stop. Here in Al's dream yard,

the light is turning, the pink of holy morning.
Seven more years of lost labour, waiting for heaven,

Jacko Jacobus squanders his cherished dream:
Rachel, the soft-eyed one, waiting for his touch.

Leah feels her womb awake
to the coming of seed.

ESCAPE

Secreted in a car trunk smelling of socks, Rachel driving
like hell across the state — the heathens watched and raved.

Jacko mingles his shit fear with black man's blood —
there is no discernible trail, just graves, makeshift graves —

and the hitman loses the scent somewhere
over the man-made lake. The swamps do the rest.

Cool Al will not slaughter family lightly,
but this is betrayal and Leah is pregnant, too.

Counting slow, he estimates his loss:
two daughters gone stupid with ungodly lust,

some grams of prime stuff, sucked up like that,
and all that loose cash, people's money, gone.

So cutting no slack is the only course,
cutting the hitman's rein, giving him rope to fly.

CADILLAC

Jacko bought himself a hopping cadillac
for five hundred dollars and two stones of crack

to nose along the autumn-orange 378
to find quiet places of greener days

in peach country Spartanburg; its hidden streets
outside the city squalor, outside the din

of midday traffic where all is quiet.
They cruised through sleepy towns, the hood a bow,

cutting new paths, new days, new dreams,
with his baby holding on to his sleeve.

They parked under some willow trees
and made love like in the movies –

slow and dizzy and all faded like –
giddy with the malt in their heads,

and they rocked to country and western tunes
coming from the radio, coming on them.

And Rachel felt naked like never before,
felt another life in this mellow grass

of splendour – sweet splendour before night
gathered them up in its blue quilt.

Is this love, this flight, this removal
to another place, another life?

The cops pulled them over on the interstate,
sniffing for dope. It's now too late for dreams.

SOUTHERN ROMANCE

While on the run from Al's hitman
  they saw things they never thought they would,

like the classic silhouette of a tree against an orange sky,
  all constructed as if with paints and false effects,

like they did on the set of *Gone with the Wind*.
  But there, somewhere outside of Greensboro,

the sky flamed like doomsday, as two lovers,
  black farming types, wrestled on a knoll

beneath an oak tree, such startling
  beauty in this half-light, when all is still.

And Jacko and Rachel sat in the grass,
  hearts swelling with the taste of magic,

while a kingfisher swooped its solitary
  flight homeward, and a cool wind

curled across the tobacco groves,
  leaves like elephants' ears, exotica along

the interstate. This love, this southern
  romantic moment, still brings tears

to Jacko's eyes, sitting in a veil of
  smoke, coughing, coughing blood while Kingston burns.

FORGIVENESS

Jacko counts the mornings in Fayettesville
waiting for the sound of death at the door.

Rachel pleads with Al, pleads for seven,
seven more years, and peace, and peace, and peace.

He's clean now, Pops. Clean as a whistle.
He's learnt his lesson well, Pops. Clean as a whistle.

And this is the love of a father; that he would lay down
the life of his hitman for his daughter, just like that.

Absolution is tossed across the swamp country,
the gun is uncocked. Jacko trembles, then breathes.

Al promises him the dignity of a country wedding
and the tender hand of his daughter to boot.

Jacko Jacobus rinses the stench of death
from his nostrils and returns to his destiny.

Amen.

SPRINGE

With Leah swelling with his first seed,
  and Becky, the mother, complaining of dreams

of marriages, births, and violent deaths,
  and Jacko embracing the brightness of love,

cruising the swamp country in his fancy cadillac
  with Rachel at his sleeve (it was all too good

for Jacko, all too sweet to last, all too pleasant,
  too right to be the path that he must take),

the call for weddings was a commandment from Al the pope,
  as compelling as any voice from the hills.

After this brief excursion from his calling,
  Jacko Jacobus girded his loins and determined

in his heart to find back the path of his destiny,
  the path to the making of his name, his legacy.

In the dark of the crack house, Al instructed Leah
  in the simple ways of winning a man's hand;

and so guided, the springe was sprung –
  Jacko Jacobus was tangled in a web of caresses.

RITUAL

Though convinced of their nomadic destiny,
Jamaican travellers often return to the soil

like instinct-driven Canadian geese,
to ritualize all stations of their living.

It was Al's desire that his daughters
return to his homeland, to find their souls,

that Leah birth, in familiar soil, children
for Jacko Jacobus the spider man.

It was Al's decree that Becky, his sister,
widowed and failing for want of her son's love,

would be at hand to bless the head of each
new infant. So, Leah would travel bethrothed

to Jacko Jacobus, seed bearer and labourer
since they had coupled already, breaking the maiden

knot, everyone knew this was so, everyone knew
it had happened before the scandalous thing with Rachel

whose mouth could not melt butter – that still-water child.
Yes, decked in the best suit Al's profits could buy,

Jacko Jacobus would return triumphant after
years sweating it out and making a name

in the swamp lands of South Carolina.
Rachel would travel as the handmaiden of her sister,

a last gift to appease the loss of her love,
a last gift to ease the pain of losing his

farmer's arms locked tight around the small of her back.
So the return to new fields in which to spawn,

to nurture. And Prospero Al, the pope of Hog Town,
orchestrated the match-making brilliance of this deal,

while Jacko Jacobus stumbled into his destiny,
doing his duty, returning to the prophecy of a mother's love.

A-SEA

The boat trundles into a vast sea of rootlessness.
　Here freedom is the absence of soil.

Jacko feels alone on the slippery deck,
　as stars like his promised descendants,

untethered by the limit of his dreams,
　dart across the black sky.

The smoke from the limping steamer's
　upturned mouth, flakes into snow,

black snow falling like bread on the water,
　undulating with news of so many shores.

Afloat on this vast fabric of green,
　Jacko believes in the impossible of heaven,

in a bright wash of light and sound,
　lifting slumbering Africa to glow – such light,

seeping pink and promising on the horizon,
　uneven like the edges of a watercolour sheet,

these soft clouds, the spread
　of colour, blue, green, red, yellow, pink,

still moving before all dries into stillness.
　Jacko sees his descendants rising, rising,

new names, new clothes, counting new beads
　on their prideful necks, new colours, new days.

RETURN (for Kamau Brathwaite)

This is the path to new life and to death,
  renaming the earth with familiar sounds,

calling, calling across the green hills
  in three-part harmony, everything jumping,

the way the snare springs you back,
  what to do but jump to the pumping sound.

This is the path by the river, now red,
  now reeking of stale bauxite,

the fish are dead, the shrimp are dead,
  the sea snake dead, the algae dead.

This is the path of new music that calls
  Africa, calls it without knowing,

the pattern of the drums on the skin.
  This is the way the snare makes you jump.

My heart beats like a baby's, alert each time
  I embrace dark nights alone.

Here in the stillness, waiting for the crack
  of something, my head pulses in fear.

Then I look for open fields away from predator
  gunman, a place to wet my body in night dew.

I have returned to plant new grass, new trees,
  and now I know I have returned knowing only

that when death comes, I will be ready,
  for home fires flame in my tender heart, my heart.

TRAVELLER

Things have not changed much.
  The treeline is almost the same.

This journey over oceans was long
  and we jettisoned much on the way,

but our eyes were never startled by the new
  light, and the earth still took to our feet.

At night I would dream it was simply
  another long march, a long trek from the disease

of the river-fly to another space, another landscape.
  Once, we walked for months, till we came to a dry place

where the earth was orange, flaming orange and dusty;
  we had never seen anything like this before.

Still, we buried our dead in the sand,
  and at night around the fire and drums

the ancestors found their way to our feet,
  to our hearts, to our livid tongues.

So this is all familiar as yesterday,
  and the yams grow large in this soil,

and my fingers still cake with the dirt,
  making tradition in new land, new spaces,

and in the sky, Nyankopon looks on
  with the same unwinking eye of the moon.

INTERLUDE

HOME MELODIES

TRICKSTER I
(For Winston Rodney)

Geriatric, wizened, ancient man
with a beard constantly damp

from the flow of good and pleasant
nectar; our cedar of Lebanon,

evergreen griot, since forever chanting
fires down below, blowing up

like volcanoes, revolution;
hearing you now chanting,

isolated prophet on the beaches,
preacher preaching on the burning shore,

yes, Winston Rodney, you could never
forget your roots, such roots,

mellow like waves along the jumping
bassline – this big sound of primordial rhythm.

Yes, if we have a true prophet,
sallow and enigmatic with grandaddy charm,

like John the Baptist with his head full of lichens,
mouth full of locusts and wildest honey;

if ever there was a prophet to walk
these blood-red streets of Kingston,

to sing travelling, travelling, we still travelling –
despite the amassed dead and the fire,

we still travelling—it is you, reggae elderman,
spear flaming through the cankered landscapes:

in the steaming clubs of Halifax,
the kerosene jazz dens of Soweto,

the red-lit drug dens of Amsterdam,
the gritty damp of London's Soho.

We believe in the words of the prophet,
transported as we are by the regal one-drop

to a time when the sea shells glinted
on the splendid Nile, blue and sparkling white.

TRICKSTER II
(For Lee "Scratch" Perry)

1

A voice cried out in the wilderness.
We all came to hear the voice

in the Cockpit valleys, to hear
the man with a skull in his hands.

He was mad.
It was all quite obvious.

We listened but saw no revelations,
just a sweet madness of new rhythms.

Afterwards, we drank mannish water,
ate curried goat, and slept peacefully.

2

Legend puts the Scratch man in trees,
comfortable in this lofty nest, where airwaves

have a clearer path to the sampling antennae
of his dangerous, bright mind.

A few were baptized to the strange
syncopations of unsteady sycophants,

but all looked to see the boy
with a sweet falsetto grained with desert grit

singing the father's songs, just as
the Scratch man prophesied would happen.

3

There would be no wailing songs
without the madness of Scratch Perry;

none of the wild weirdness of *Kaya*,
none of the leap of images, enigmatic

mysteries like scripture; none of the miracle
of guitars twined each on each,

without this man, with his fired
brain and fingers of brilliant innovation

tweaking the nine-track sound board,
teasing out new ways to see heaven.

There would be nothing of the crucifixion,
no resurrection repeated each time another

reggae operator is born, again, again,
no revolution without this locust-eating prophet.

4

All that is left is his bodiless head
chatting, chatting, tongue like a flapping bell,

tongue among the teeth. Salome too is dead,
but the head still creates this twisted

sound here on Switzerland's slopes.
Rastaman defies the chill and prophecies,

his head on a compact disc like a platter
spinning, spinning, spinning, new sounds.

TRICKSTER III

This bassline is sticky like asphalt
and wet like molasses heated nice and hot,

and the bass drum booms my heart,
jumping me, jump-starting me

to find the path of this sluggish sound;
I follow the tap like a tick catching light

in its rainbow gossamer wings
on top of a big ear elephant;

I follow the pluck of a mute lead-guitar string,
tacking, tacking out a tattoo to the bassline;

I let the syrup surround my legs
and my waist is moving without a cue,

without a clue of where we are going,
walking on the spot like this.

Coolly, deadly, roots sound on my back,
and I can conjure hope in anything;

dreams in my cubby hole of a room where
the roaches scuttle from the tonguing gekko.

This music finds me giddy and centered, but when
morning comes, I am lost again, no love, just lost again.

TRICKSTER IV
(For Sister Patra)

Surfing on the dance floor,
balancing that cut of wave,

missing brilliant coral with
a slash and sway of my arm,

watch me fall back, fall back,
then wheel and come again,

something catching me with
invisible hands on the down beat.

Rapid is the chant of the microphone
queen with lyrics like a whip,

lashing me with her rhythm,
then balming me with a sweet

soprano sounding like sticky
on the bubbly bassline.

Sometimes the honey mellows in my soul
and melts my knees to water

and it's a sea surf teasing the sand
back and forth, making froth.

This, this, dis ya sound sweet
you see, sweet like sugar and lime.

Limbo is the way to limber,
seeming to fall back with my arms,

then catch me back with propeller action,
this is the Bogle at work, ya,

on the undulating salt deck of our days
to the sound we lost so long ago

when we left the kraal, leaving no forwarding
address, just forwarding to another rock.

But this echo of a land, a land
so far, so far, across the sea,

is lashed to the shock of this lyrical feast,
riding this sweet rhythmic beat.

Somebody say—Vershan!—and then hear
the drum in the sister's tongue,

playing like a gospeller to the wash
of the four-part harmony, dripping sex –

and the way I feel is wild;
wilding up myself with eyes open wide,

surfing on the dance floor
surfing on the dance floor.

And when she's done her lyrical jam
this rest is like old, old, old, sleep

after sweating sea water, spilling sea water
flowing like that and falling: HEAVY!

PART TWO

ROCK-STONE

KINGSTON HARBOUR

There is in Jacko's head an old memory
of a chaotic storm, flailing the Jamaican hills

with knife blades of lightning and a silver
tumble of rain, pelting everything, pelting

him, beating his cowered head. And standing,
soaked to the skin, his neck veins jumping,

his hands gnarled with labour and seasoned
with the blood of slaughtered game,

his brows dripping like waterfalls
over his eyes, was Eric, disenfranchised,

staring after Jacko fleeing into the night;
Becky weeping, trying to shade her head

from the deluge with an old *Gleaner*, trying to
stay Eric's righteous hand, curled around the basic

wood of the machete, with her eyes, her eyes only.
Death, pale and bloodless, whispered among the trees,

and Jacko recalls the daring of Eric's
unflinching eyes. This memory returns

like seasonal storms, as clamorous
August's tropical depressions drive Jacko

and his sac full of blessed seed
into Kingston's harbour, then a slippery

point of departure, the sea, a buffer
against the coming of night, of dark night.

Now, Jacko stands staring into the island,
his back to the sea, his eyes cooled by the shadowing

hills, the purple hills of Blue Mountain
shrouded in gray. He smiles at the way

the city glows against the ashen sky.
Jacko barrels gifts for his brother.

A peace offering to calm the years of resentment.
He can tell it will not be enough, not enough at all.

THE MESSAGE

1

The news of Jacko's arrival is whispered;
the helper is afraid to pass on the message

to stoic Eric, whose wife, Judith, does not offer
to speak, gruffly dismisses the helper's anxiety,

then vanishes into the safety of her room
long before the embers of daylight dim,

before the return of Eric from his ordered
routines in the belly of Kingston.

2

The helper watches Eric stare into the flickering
gaudy of Kingston, a stark wind off the hills.

He is sucking his teeth, pulling at the goat
wedged somewhere between molar and incisor.

She does not speak. The clatter of dishes,
the hum of a dirge. The waiting.   Rock.   Hard place.

3

The rumours of a tragic wedge between
the brothers have always been whispered

from gardener to helper to cook to nanny.
Eric bears a secret of blood that everyone

knows – they know why he hardly ever smiles
as he stiffly traverses the avenue to the corner

for his transport out. The news of Jacko's return will,
she knows, unsettle the comfort of his simple life.

The cricket's call rises and falls in the dusk.
Death smells like the dank upturned earth

of this land carved into the hill,
like a tomb, a resting place for the weary.

4

A message come say a man want to see yuh,
Say is yuh bredda, come from foreign.

He gazes at her, not reading the code of syntax.
Then she sees the flicker of acknowledgment –

it is a wince, a twitching of the flesh
beneath the eye, a jump of the jaw – he turns.

She can hear the uneven of his breathing,
as his eyes devour the jeweled basin below.

She backs away, unable to turn, watching
the way his body grows rigid, cold, dead.

EMBRACE

But Esau ran to meet Jacob and embraced him; he threw his
arms around his neck and kissed him. And they wept. (Genesis)

I embrace with tears the return of my sorrow,
    I welcome my cerasee of lament;

I had forgotten for too long the taste of life,
    the hyssop of my existence.

My woe arrives uncertain of my disposition;
    he is not sure I will fight it,

he cannot tell from the smile on me
    so he tests the waters – I can see

the trick glint in his eyes; he is not sure
    he can charm me with smiles;

it is hard to believe we fed from the same
    coiled umbilical of our mother.

I embrace him; I embrace my father's shadow,
    I embrace the memory of loss,

I embrace him; I can feel the old pattern
    return; my body is mine again, broken.

It is the way of this world, it is
    the path back to my wounded truer self.

PARTING WAYS

Esau said, *I will walk with you*
the arduous journey back to our new home.

Jacob said, *My people are weighed down*
with infants, young calves. Go ahead, I follow.

Esau said, *I will leave some with you*
to guide and guard on the path to our new home.

Jacob said, *We will linger too much, tire*
your people unduly. No, no, go ahead, I follow.

Esau said, *I long for the time we may plant*
our nations side by side, blood by blood in our new home.

Jacob smiled his spider smile, thinking, *I see*
daggers in your eyes, all treachery – go ahead, I follow.

And Esau went ahead rejoicing at the return
of his blood, his hope, his pain, his being.

At the fork of the road, Jacob stared at the path
left by Esau; he turned away from it, winking at the sun.

HOW THE WEDDING LAUGHED

In the red dirt of St Elizabeth
a pig was slaughtered and a goat,

a pit dug deep and filled with coals
to roast the sow, to roast the goat.

And how the wedding laughed.
The virgins, jealous in their Sunday best,

compared their breasts and hips
with Leah's proud strut and grin,

and how the wedding laughed.
The rum flowed through the night,

the pot of curried goat had no bottom,
and feast, they feasted till daylight came;

yes, how the wedding laughed.
And Leah let her lips be kissed

by an old boyfriend, a cop,
giddy with the sight of her vulnerable white,

her ebony skin all slick with sweat,
her eyes all wet with the stir of rum.

Her lips parted and she bit his tongue
and the people giggled and whispered;

yes, how the wedding laughed.
But Jacko, indulgent, smiled it off

and drank some more, and more, and more
then fell on Rachel's breasts in tears.

Man, how the wedding laughed!
Yes, how the wedding laughed!

AFTER CONSUMMATION

After long years
of slicking his palms

with spit and groans of shame,
spilling his precious seed

like Onan among
the sterile stones,

the mud of an open-legged woman
can make you blind.

Who can see when all there is
is feel; can hear when breathing is all?

It is only after the coming and the rest,
when light stirs the sleeping two

that he sees his lover
to be another, not the dream,

not the woman
he has loved

those cool mornings on the hill,
howling his ejaculations to the sky.

SECOND MONTH

Like a wind-ravaged sapling,
  folded at the waist, undulating,

is Leah in a white shift
  heaving up so much good food

by the standpipe on this ash-gray
  morning. She has not bled again

and everything about her is touchy,
  sensitive to each wind's breath. The barren

guinep tree shudders over her.
  Rachel gazes through the mesh

of her caged room, chicken glass
  eye softening with loose water.

In months there will be another,
  another anchor to Jacko's fleet foot,

another stone to swallow.
  Calmly wiping a trail of spittle,

Leah unfolds, clutching her waist
  and breathes into the dawn.

In her heart, Rachel longs
  to feel the heaviness of new life;

Jacko's seed fleshing, fleshing
  in the silence of still, leaf-green mornings.

MOTHER LOAD

How much easier it is to fly
  into the deepening blue

without the weight of a baby
  drawing down, drawing down.

We are remaking my husband in me
  as an anchor, a way to hold him here,

but I can fly no more
  drawn down by this heaviness.

How much easier it is to dance
  on tiled floors, making wind on my face,

without the weight of this growth
  in my womb, drawing me, drawing me.

I have learnt to take pride
  in the ripeness of my breasts,

in the fertile soil I give him,
  to take small pleasures in his glory,

but I can dance no more
  drawn down by this heaviness.

These days, I count in years
  not months, not weeks –

years: from crawl to walk,
  to sleep through the night,

to pull-ups not diapers and then briefs,
   to a way of saying no that he will understand,

to the first abandonment to others,
   to decades away when man will be his name –

and maybe then, my bones will still be supple
   enough to catch the curve of wind, and fly.

TENANTS

Tenants of wood and mesh
and a broad sloping galvanize roof

sheltered by a barren guinep tree
that sheds her brittle leaves like tears;

partitioned into a dank washroom
where Leah and Rachel bleach

the expensive whites of the budding middle-class,
collected each Monday in Hope Pastures and the hills,

treading up the softening asphalt and gravel
sweat and silence, sweat and silence, from gate to gate;

partitioned into permeable cubicles
where sounds of love penetrate,

and babies can be heard whimpering, wailing,
noses stuffed with drying colds –

the sound like a constant weight of regret
over Rachel's well-manicured head and face.

The backyard is the kitchen
where dry bones, chewed and left by the dogs,

jut from the stony earth as from bursting graves,
and herbs and weeds wrestle around the rusting fence.

At night the sound of a preacher on the transistor
hangs like a mist in the pale lamplight,

and mosquitoes defy the stench of kerosene smoke,
multiplying themselves in the standing pools of the yard.

LONGING

Reading the yellowing leaves of scripture,
  cocooned in the soft quiet of night,

Rachel dreams of love, its treachery
  like the terrible warmth of stolen embraces.

Rachel sees Jacko, bandy-legged and tough,
  kicking stones on the marl road,

waiting for the bossman, foreman to come
  in his red pick-up with promise of work.

Rachel sees Jacko dragging a slaughtered predator crow
  from the edge of the ponds of rainbow trout,

while its mates circle in the blue beyond and wait
  to scatter the flies from the drying blood.

In this she sees the written hand of God
  guiding her in her quiet time of revelations.

Rachel sees Jacko making his seed froth,
  planting it in shallow soil, and gloating Leah

pat-patting his back, the smell of light
  perfume and Limacol in the air.

Rachel prays the prayer of impossible love:
  of fate, of God's wisdom, dead wives, lonely widowers,

comforting Jacko Jacobus in his grief –
  all this in the scriptures like prophecy in the wind.

BIRTHING ROOM

There is much white in the birthing room,
the purest light from the brilliant day.

She had stood and finished the stew peas and rice
and walked in the sun through bright contractions.

Now propped like a queen on cushions of white
Leah's crown of unruly hair spreads like water.

The midwife, starched to severe purity,
commands the ritual of birthing

with silver and bright steel instruments,
prodding, feeling, squeezing, looking.

Push... now... push... now... push... Wait.
Push... yuh not breathing, chile... Bear down! Wait!

And Leah floats in a cloud of
white pain until the howl shatters

the coming down of everything wet,
everything flowing river-wet, down.

The boy is swaddled in white
and named softly, named for a mountain.

His eyes tight, conceal the blade of his future,
the blood red of so much blood shed by his hand.

But quiet is the light on this bright
day when babies are soft as cotton.

Leah dreams of clouds and clouds
swimming in the brilliance of blue.

DRIZZLE

1

Not dew but light rain slicks the day.
  O the mountains leap and clap their hands.

Grey in the hills, a coal fire slumbers
  and day breaks lazily shedding the lingering fog.

Jacko Jacobus smells the mellow of steamed ackee
  over the tart of stale urine warming.

A dog slinks into the trees, rheumy eyed.
  A rooster alarms nonchalant in the sifted sunlight.

2

Not dew but light rain greens the leaves
  and the bones repeat the ritual of rising,

slower now, cracking. Leah has coughed
  her slack body awake to boil saltfish in the gloom.

Rachel sips the air, succulent, soft,
  her breasts exposed to the half light.

Yuh gone...? From the syrup of sleep.
  Ah gone... Jacko Jacobus droops into the rain.

3

The mini-van smells of ackee and fish.
  Jacko chews dreamily, eating from aluminium foil.

The city awakes like a sheet of startled
  flies leaving a bloated carcass.

Jacko's machete's pressed hard on his thigh,
  sun is his task master, whip, his boss.

PSALM 36

Even at night, laid out as in a coffin,
    he can't sleep for the evil in his heart;

he is weaving baskets to catch fish
    swimming home in fish water;

that is the sinfulness of the wicked;
    and his wife does not know

why he turns and turns all night,
    mouth muttering as if there are pebbles in his heart.

There is an oracle in my heart
    tells me to speak like this;

but I am not a prophet, just a player
    of songs, a lyrics man, with two sacs

of blessed seed to spawn a generation
    of miracle-makers. My task is just to plow the earth,

plant my seed and then, like some ephemeral
    insect, become one with the mist.

But I know the wicked man and his works,
    know his cunning machinations that seem

so gloriously brilliant in their diabolic wit
    here in the light of day. But who would

guess the planning he does deep in the night
    tossing on the fetid damp of his sepulchral sheets?

For a thirsting man caught here, stranded
  late at night between two dry hills,

to have my prayers answered is to taste sweet water,
  and the passing of fear — fear of the drawn gun

ready to spill my simple brains
  on this cooking tarmac; fear of the old ghosts

rising from the sea with their unknowable
  anger, ready to strike me dumb, dry my seed —

the passing of such fears brings cool calm breezes
  to my soul, and I know that the sound

of gigantic wings flapping is
  a sign of the love of heaven.

Few songs but these tried and proven
  hymnals of majestic patience can

sing the largeness of my gratitude
  in these dark times. Continue your wash

of love for my seed and their seed;
  bring stones to crush the blundering heads

of my enemies, and may the heart of the sweating,
  evil man, seeping all that pig flesh,

stop so sudden with startle and dread,
  never to start again, never to start again.

VISITATION

Slaughtering fire ants: he is consumed
by the planning of their efficient genocide

each waking hour, each silent moment
chewing on his meal, shitting in the bush,

treading each day along the marl road,
dreaming of new richness to come,

as if a victory over this pestilence
will be a sign that the tide has turned for him;

no more stone and dry dry bread,
no more counting pennies.

There is a passion that takes hold of him,
a madness for meticulous precision

as he chuckles at the trickery of spreading
fine white cornmeal over the sandy mounds.

Their thirst after the gluttonous feeding
will cause the flour to swell until they pop

and rot, fermenting the underearth with the smell
of minerals. And the earth will green in their wake.

One day as he stared into the pattern
of white on the sandy mounds,

an angel appeared unto Jacko Jacobus
while he stood with his home-made hoe,

and promised him children like sands
and a history to be read by generations.

Then calmly the angel left,
leaving a soft scent of incense.

Standing in the sudden silence,
Jacko could hear the ants multiplying.

PENIEL

In a dream, a wide-hipped woman
with coal-black skin and eyes like embers,

identifies the lanky, sloping man approaching,
dangling arms and fingernails stained with old blood

as an angel; a walking spirit on his
way to other destinations. Jacko trembles at the sight.

These days he sees the blank gaze of Eric
in the pattern of the sky. He can feel the way his breath

rattles his chest. There has been no news
of his brother's feelings. Jacko fears the worst.

The lanky man will not stop, though Jacko
screams him to halt. The coal-black woman loses

control; she stutters, she can feel the unseating
of calm in the man she has called an angel – smells the blood

seeping like sweat from his armpits. She has
no assurances for Jacko who struts, circles, jeering the angel,

naming him brother, twin, soul-mate; deaf
to her reasoning. Jacko pushes, the angel falls.

Jacko gloats; then the red hands pull Jacko
into the dust. The night turns in on itself, their

breathing pulsing in the darkness. The angel tries
to go, crippling Jacko on the hip. The tentacle

arms of Jacko hold on: *Forgive me, forgive me,*
Eric; Jesus God, man, yuh mus' forgive me, Eric!

Clumsily, the angel passes a dusty hand over
Jacko's balding pate. The sun has started to smile

behind the cliffs; there is nothing left for the angel
to do. Jacko falls away weeping. *Thank yuh, Thanks.*

Leah gathers his head to her breasts
stroking the sweat and torment in his flesh.

Mawning, Jacko, is mawning now. Is alright.
The rooster begins the relay of alarums.

Jacko rises slowly, his body bruised with sleep.
Leah can see the limp in his dragging feet.

CANTINA

The Chinese proprietor calls it a cantina
from the country song on the radio,

but all they sell is grocery things,
carbolic soap, seed and stink salt fish.

His anaemic looking wife sings nasally
while stirring aromas, so exotic, so sweet,

in the wok for the lunch-hour meals
she makes each day and sells for a pittance.

Here is where Jacko eats among the flies
dancing around the salt pork and flour,

listening to the whine of her singing,
making him cry sometimes for lost homes.

Sometimes, vulnerable like this,
as if called by his weeping and falling heart,

the slick-haired, red-boned girl appears,
all in white, boots, pants so tight, teeth bright,

announcing her entrance from far away,
Miss Chin! to Mrs Ping, who nods

and maybe smiles without turning, still singing,
stewing the fried balls in the plum syrup.

Jacko looks at her with his water eyes
and sometimes when she is not in a hurry

she follows him chewing into the yard in the back
where love is never made, just fire,

to the nasal cry of the Chinese woman,
her eyes dripping, her voice sharply rising.

MANDRAKE

1

The earth tilts,
  all light is a blur of memory.

The rum makes him careless;
  the perfumed powder of her smile

and the slant of her body,
  because one leg is shorter,

making her breasts move,
  jiggling each time she steps,

draws his straying eye to it all,
on Matilda's Corner where everything strays.

After, her smell clings to his skin.
  At home, Leah waits hungry

for the jerk pork he stepped out to get,
  so hungry her head is light,

while the baby tosses and flops.
  When he comes there is a woman's smell

on him; this smell like her own shame
  Leah smells on him with his empty hands,

and it flames her weary mind.
  Jacko fumbles with words, then slumps down,

her words raining like stones
   on his adulterer's head in the lamplight.

2

Rachel finds scowling Leah
   rocking with belly pain,

the hunger and the grief
   slapping her strained ribs

as she sits on the rough cement stair.
   Rachel carries her aluminum foil

warm with fried rice, jerk and greasy bread,
   and a frosty gill of Irish Moss slippery in her hand.

Yuh want 'im? Eh? Yuh want dat piece a shit?
   Well, yuh can 'ave 'im. Everybody else done get 'im,

after all... Jus give me de food
   and de Irish Moss, das all, das all...

A simple transaction is made.
   Leah swallows quickly without chewing

Miss Ping's spicy rice and meat;
   Rachel, in the backroom, coaxes some firmness

in this flaccid man, grunting,
   moving by instinct, coming

soundless with a sigh,
   the moon silvering their coupling.

Yuh done? Ah ready fe sleep now.
 'Im do anyt'ing doh? Come, come...

Rachel scrambles in quiet shame,
  gathering her clothes and leaving

past Leah who sways in the moonlight,
  eyes dull and dry with nothing,

her mouth shiny with the grease
  of the jerk and fried rice. Jacko is a lump.

Nice rice. Nice rice. Leah rubs the taut
  of her belly and lays her body down.

Rachel listens to V.T. Williams
  filling up the midnight with fire gospel,

gravel and sparks from a throat
  that has taken this path too many times.

A voice speaks: *Shall be blessed*
 your womb shall be blessed, barren child.

A wind stirs the guinep tree's leaves.
  An owl hoots the coming of prophecy –

Leah dreams of their mother's funeral,
  and the shroud of white she wore.

LION HEART

Showing love under the soft lamplight,
  cradling his slumbering head in her thighs,

Rachel uses her sensitive soft fingertips
  to find the roundness of ripe pimples,

squeezing lines of pale yellow,
  sweet satisfaction of popped bumps.

And even after all oil and matter
  has been drawn out, she caresses

the slack face of Jacko Jacobus,
  putting dreams into his lidded eyes,

putting love into the rugged curve
  of his lump of nose, the roughness of his chin,

the severe scars of his broken lips,
  the stone of his tight leather forehead;

like feeling the shape of the found skull
  of some long forgotten ancestor.

Showing love like this,
  she sings soft, *fi mi love 'ave lion heart...*

BARREN

At first the labouring is earnest,
their heat spent in sweat-soaked sheets,

the violence of her demanding,
drawing, drawing him to bursting

is a strange aphrodisiac
a way to keep on wanting it.

At first her skin is fallow,
leaping like sprouting grass,

breaking seeds, splitting at the touch,
giving dew in the morning light.

Then dryness cakes the flesh,
cracks the supple skin, now leather.

Nothing has changed, but time has passed
and nothing grows here it seems – everything dies.

The panting is routine, toil,
quick, not too soon, never too soon to sleep.

This barrenness is like a curse,
as if love so impossible can only give

deserts of stark emptiness.
While in the other room,

a reluctant tossed kiss germinates,
fermenting sperm and egg,

making all soft and full
despite the dry lovelessness

of the land. This cruel
irony is a stone in the throat,

a way to make the proud humble,
to bring tears for past sins.

MEDITATING

Night is a symphony of mad crickets,
  croaking lizards on the branches of trees.

The solitary outside street lamp,
  fed by the humming generator in the room

above the cafeteria, filters the moon blue,
  like spilt milk, on the lawn. It is a point

of meditation for Jacko Jacobus
  as he counts his curses – seven years of ill luck.

Moths and flying ants dart dizzily
  around the glow – it will soon rain .

Some fall and shed their wings, become mortal,
  speak no words given to them by God. Gekkos crawl

into the wash of light, heads bobbing;
  they swallow these insects and run.

This climb and descent on a ladder
  of borrowed electric light calls to memory

an old dream of impossible tenacity
  in Jacko's ailing head. But this is no

shrine to the spoken words of angels,
  to the contract of blood and spirit,

to the mounds of flat stones
  piled high beside silent streams;

just a misplaced street lamp lighting nothing
  but a useless circle of grass.

No miracle in this apparition.
  Morning, too, will come without fanfare.

COVENANT
(for Michelle)

Stone in water,
  pile the stones.

Stone in my heart,
  heart is water.

There is a pillar where we stopped
  and found love by a stream,

where we drank sweetly and rested
  while the sun washed the tree tops.

Pillar of our journey, smooth flat stones
  taken from the cool of streams.

This is the promise of our many journeys,
  hands clasped, faces looking away.

My island is a monument of love;
  stone is water, jam-rock is the promised

hope of these dark times, my love,
  but I feel your water caressing stone

and I am washed, washed by your
  love, stone in water on this island

green with the long caress of
  water on the constant stone.

My heart is water
  heart of stone, always adamant.

WASH BELLY

It is for no other reason but this one
overreaching truth, that all things must be said

at least once – spoken and then tugged
dancing in the wind, before cutting the string,

letting the thought go to the bluest of skies,
then gone forever – the spoken unspoken.

Here is what this poem must dare to speak
to say, maybe, that Benny the wash belly

did murder her, Jacko's heart's solace,
his cherished sunset on the St. Elizabeth plains,

his bright streak of crimson love
flaming his darker days; though to say

that Benny, the prettiest eyes of all,
in his wailing arrival, stopped her breath,

so beautiful was his blood-slick head,
and murdered her with love, is hard.

Afterwards, Jacko wept, knowing too well
he had loved her too much for her to live

beyond this miracle of Benny's coming,
for with God, such sweet moments of light

are punishable by death and profoundest loss.
He knew and rued the day he held her

and whispered *I love you more than Him*.
And there lies Rachel wrestling in the bed

of slippery fluids, slipping, slipping, then
gone. The midwife covered her bleeding womb,

then lingered beneath the guinep tree
dragging cigarette after cigarette

in silence. Now all that is left is regret
for having said this thing – this truth:

Benny murdered his mother with his arrival.
I have said this for Jacko Jacobus

who sits and stares into the wind,
feeling the way the poem beats his heart.

IN MEMORIAM

All that is left of her,
   all that remains after the wailing

for nine nights in a mist of rum,
   all that is left after the jealous eye

of Leah lamented Jacko's second death
   for this his lost dream, all that is left

of delicate Rachel with bones catching light
   on her upturned face, all that is left

is the memory of her part in this chain
   of generations, the sacrifice of her womb,

her body, her soul to continue this chain
   of generations; the scabs on her feet

from walking so many miles to sustain the chain
   of generations; the puckered fingers and varicose

veins to make ends meet, to carry out the living
   for the birthing of her children, his children.

All that remains is a mound where she was laid,
   and in the sky sometimes, there are colours

that she once saw and swam among, way up there in
   swamp country where her first woman's blood

was poured; in that sky, there is the smell
   of magnolia and jasmine, and the thick of swamp,

and then the wind stirs and blows all that away,
   till all that is left is a simple longing

in Jacko's falling heart,
   in Jacko's failing heart.

LOW COUNTRY

And when nine nights had passed, Rachel took flight,
  alighting on the land of her navel string.

Born in the low country,
  coming home is back to thick green,

and the soil enriched with the bones
  of old travellers, deposited on this soft earth,

where the water settles so close to the surface
  you smell her dank and feel her chill;

and all the tears, all the songs of lost homes,
  all the libations poured to broken gods,

to the memory of the tender kraal,
  the dance of the mothers in the sunset,

the age mates whose circumcision blood
  tied them in mythic oneness,

all this is caught in the rich alluvia
  of old gospel songs, and settles in the gaze

of a black woman burdened with age,
  walking the darkly meandering roads

of this low country, where low riding is the way.
  Poor, but this is all the home she's got.

Arriving in the low country, the thick
  green mellows like tobacco fields

in the fallen sun—she breathes
  in the dank of memory: home, home.

GROUNDSMAN

When the transparent-skinned
St. Andrew accents came with papers

and prospector's tripods and armed guards
to claim the land, Jacko wept.

My sister dead, now,
an' yuh done murder mi daughter

an' de odder is nutting but a tiaad horse
so yuh deh 'pon yuh own, now, Jacko. . .

was the way it was put in the missive Al
sent third class mail from Sumter city.

When they slaughtered the long nurtured crop
and fired the house of wood and mesh,

Jacko wept. When the flattened, barren lot,
where schoolboys had galloped their horses,

howling at the rush of trees,
as they ducked the low-hanging limbs,

would not give forth fruit
to feed the hungry children,

all six with eyes as deep and old
as history, Jacko wept.

Then gathering his mettle, and pushed by
Leah's pragmatic nagging,

he picked up a rake and pushed a barrow
into the boy's school, where chalkdust

hung like a cloud, and asked the headmaster
for a pittance for clearing the leaf-strewn yards.

And there among the pyres of raked leaves
Jacko dreamt of castles of glory and wept.

OCCUPATION

Jacko made a living by selling the boys
Panther condoms, tattered *Hustler* magazines;

by managing the dark screening room
where his enterprising sons made good nickel

showing blue movies – all pink and red
with white folks being nasty – to boys

hungry for a way out of the growing madness
of their awakened libidos. Jacko would be lookout.

Jacko made a living by cherishing
the secrets of teachers who rendezvoused at night

in the dark schoolyard while the world and their
spouses dreamed; by carrying secret messages,

decrepit Eros, with his squeaking barrow,
mediating love for a favour or two,

silent, unquestioning go-between.
At night, Jacko listened to old arias

on his scratching gramophone, cloistered
in his other world, while the city crumpled around him;

he listened to Kamau Brathwaite calling Africa
on a fine recording, a gift from a teacher who did get caught.

Jacko dreamt of the Nile and camels,
of his lost progeny – his blessed sons

strutting like forceripe pimps, cruising the city
with surefooted grace, making deals

with political types, casual violence in their eyes.
Still, no one starved, no one thirsted,

no one wanted for hearth or home,
and his daughters learnt grace and algebra

and talked of university and degrees
with three square meals a day.

SHECHAM

1

Waiting for Carib's gates to open,
squeezed tight like this, groin to ass,

their eyes, as they say, made four –
not quite love, but there was his slow gaze,

his casual and lofty oversight of all he surveyed,
standing in the dusk above Cross Roads

with its chaos of mini buses and jolly-buses,
with its youth vendors shouting out their wares,

and the way he whistled an old mento tune,
a tune for a grandfather sitting on a country porch

watching the sea; even in this din
she heard his sweet sound when their eyes,

as they say, made four. But how else must love
begin, and anyway, he made her laugh,

with his funny faces and his bullying of his boys,
who simply loved their leader in his dapper threads.

So she did not have to push and sweat, wrestle and bore
to get into the theatre this time. No, this time

she joined the respectable class of box-seaters
and saw the film in soft, red-cushioned comfort.

Taking her home in his old man's Volvo,
through lanes she had never seen before,

the street lights spreading before them like flowers,
guiding their path to some pleasant place,

she let the music from his sound system
suck her deep into the soft of his car,

fluting melodies on a syrup reggae beat –
Herbie Mann, who she had never heard before,

seducing her lithe body into complete trust.
When she was close to home, she lied

and pointed up into the hills where the houses
glowed white in the moonlight, *Let me off there...*

He smiled and swung instead up Hope Road
into Hope Gardens where they ate barbecued

chicken dripping with sweet and tart,
and sipped cool beer and laughed like that.

Then he pushed his sticky hands into her crotch
without question, excuse me, or please, may I,

and plucked her virgin self all bloody
and whimpering no in the naked night;

and how she cried for eating the chicken,
for sinking into the flute and bass of his eyes.

He discarded her on the side of Hope Road,
annoyed at her whimpering and ingratitude,

bright lights piercing her from all sides,
still dizzy with not knowing how it all began,

dragging her self back to the squalid yard
where the gramophone wailed its arias.

3

From whisperings with Leah, her mother,
to the detailed account to her father,

the household swelled with resolve. Jacko
planned his grief perfectly, no tears until her brothers,

his sons, arrived to hear the tale.
Then he let his heart fall, his head fall,

his body stumbled like death to the soil,
and the boys watched in silence.

4

The Syrian boy, whose sloe eyes, now trapped,
are the eyes of a youth whose martyrdom

could spawn a cult of believers,
spilling flowers and prayers for his blessing

upon the bowed heads of broken-hearted lovers;
those eyes dart about for escape,

surrounded as he was by this gathering of families,
as if someone was dead or dying.

Riding through the bush and bramble with his family
to the shack where she lived; he knew he had been tricked

for this was no mansion glowing ivory-white on the hill,
no splendid wealth to suit his sweet tooth.

He felt the shame of his father's eyes
and the gasp at the shock in his mother's breath

when they saw the hugeness of the barren guinep tree
dwarfing the home of Dinah, his erstwhile lover,

and he hoped for a feud, a family dispute,
a way to walk from this single, intact.

So he confessed, almost certain that his disdain
for the family standing before the shack,

watching the caravan of spanking new Volvos,
would be his father's, his mother's, his brothers'.

But in the half-light of the innards of the shack,
trapped by the dignity and grace of her gentle voice,

he confessed again, not through fear or bravado,
but because a lie in the face of Dinah's calm account,

a lie in the face of her precise logic of rape, abuse,
callousness, would surely have fallen on deaf ears.

She was, after all, too beautiful and calm,
too brilliant with books and responsible charm

to make up a lie like this. And all who sat here
understood this, so what else was there to do but confess?

So he did – his father slapping him on the back
assuring him that it could have been worse.

She could have been ugly and stupid and expensive,
what with the fares to get one from New York or Toronto;

and anyway, he liked the black ones,
wasn't that what he often said?

Jacko Jacobus sat silent, rueing the insult
of this forceripe union, so well organised by his sons

who had not reached, like warriors, for machetes
to slaughter this whistling boy and his sloe eyes.

But here was the way of the world, the boys
are men, he thought, and she is their sister.

It was all rum and curry while the women
whispered in the yard. The men

muttered at the righteousness of this union –
Dinah to finish school and maybe more,

while the boy watched his path crumbling
before him, everything like a dream.

5

Come midnight, Jacko yawned and excused himself.
The brothers promised more rum on Red Hills Road.

How could the Syrians deny their new family
its rituals of welcome: the acrobatic pelvis

of a coal-black woman dancing to the syrup bassline
around a stiff pole, there in the middle of the stage,

undulating with impossible gyrations; or the giving
flesh of thousand-dollar prostitutes with flame-red lips;

the liquor, the weed, the pleasurable illicitness of it all –
how could they refuse such simple acts of gratitude?

And so they fell into the softness of these offerings,
each to his own destiny in the dark thighs

of the Pussy Den on Red Hills Road,
while the music shuddered the earth dully.

6

It was buried somewhere on the third page,
near the news of falling currency rates

and the pictures of ribbon-cuttings by bleary eyed
political types, this discovery of a family of men

bleeding from wounds to their sacred parts
in the cheap perfume of a prostitute's sheets;

naked, robbed, tied and gagged, no clues,
just caught in mid breath, while the crowd gathered.

Dinah was bundled into a waiting jet
and flown to Miami, while everyone laughed.

But Jacko wept at the news of his daughter's spoilt marriage.
He spoke no words for months so much he missed her.

UNTITLED

The wind lashes its tail;
  brown leaves break free from the pile

and dance around Jacko's
  slanted, still body, eyes all hollow,

hand on chin, looking
  far into the pale blue,

sucking soft on a cigarette
  making mist like heaven's avenue.

The doctor has warned him off
  with horror stories of tightening chest, hardening veins,

talking like a real estate agent
  about building a new edifice of health

for a longer life, a longer life
  in this dumb daze of his last days.

Jacko always nods in patient abeyance,
  then lights up in the parking lot.

The wind calms the coughing.
  The leaves wait trembling for stillness to fall.

Sunlight catches the silver of the pond,
  a netting of light over the green of weeds.

FALTER

Eric is counting the scattered seed of Jacko.
The numerology is astounding.

He can field a coed cricket eleven,
plus twelfth man and waterboys.

In the future some will wonder at history.
Eric, the red-eyed, will surely be

a fallen villain in the narrative,
the one who could not see with eyes of angels,

nor hear the voice of God in the heavens.
He will be the tangent, the margin,

a generation of relations grafted to the living tree.
There are too many children now blooming life

despite their clandestine making; some call
Jacko lucky, as if that is consolation. To die

embracing the treachery of fate is to die defeated.
Eric clutches himself at night and weeps.

TRICKSTER

Every trick executed with that flick of my wrist,
every deft sleight of hand by me, Jacobus,

was a way to prepare the language of my path,
a way to tell how I would be met on the road.

My way was made by a winking of the eye,
for my way was perilous and the rocks were large;

and though I know that I made my bed of woes,
there was an urge to live beyond the moment,

to survive the onslaught of time's wrath,
to make it to the other side, intact, if

somewhat tarnished by the journey.
This tracing of my many journeys,

stretches out like delicate parchment.
The roads are strewn with piles of stones

for each successful trick, each quick
foot-shuffle, working my magic like that.

And God is my light and salvation,
not because of the purity of my soul,

(that was too long ago, and besides,
I was too young to take credit for it),

but because of the prophecy of his own mouth.
Beyond me, beyond my ways, beyond it all,

there is an inexorable end he has made,
warts, deceptions, slow tongues, lies, and all.

This was the path made before me:
I bore seed to make nations tremble,

me, unworthy trickster, with too little faith
to depend on the miracle of God – I, Jacobus

made my own paths, and now swallow the bitter weed
of my fallen ways. It is faithlessness, but it is so

when you have been called to this walk of destiny;
it is all you can do to remain awake

for the fanfare and the tributes at the end of the way,
it is all you can do to be human again, it is all.

FAITH

Every creator is a trickster.
  Every progenitor is a wit-man.

Grey like this, I look dull;
  it has been a long, long time

since my faithless hurtle into adventure,
  making this history of impossible progeny,

making the sky explode in blue and white,
  with silken scatterings of delicate lines

like the broken strings of stitched flesh.
  It was I who made that sky expand to bursting;

this is what I believed in my faithless heart,
  but that was a long time ago, and besides,

the folks are all dead,
  and the earth has moved on.

Now grey and faithful, I watch for the coming of rain
  in season, in time; for the coming of Sahara sands

on the belly of the Atlantic winds, in season,
  in time – these miracles; I watch with knowing

boredom spinning leaves, for this is the way of the Lord,
  this predictable calm of each new morning,

this is the way of the Lord. I watch the slowing
  of my bones, the collapsing of my blackening lungs,

the dying of my memory – these things I know
  to be the way of the Lord, the way of my journey

to that heaven of blue and streaks of white,
  the boredom of faithfulness, nothing left

for the wizardry of my wit, as I watch the leaves
  shed themselves and fall, falling down,

as I watch my daughters multiply themselves,
  my sons wreak havoc on the nations.

There is nothing new in the will of the Almighty;
  with faith all things are painfully possible,

with faith all things must be.
  Then I will lie and rest my bones,

retired trickster, joker, magic-maker,
  retired into the quiet of belief in mornings.

BLESSED

The blessing of God is an intangible
as trustworthy as myth – a new day in the clamour

of traffic, smoke and the acrid remnants
of stray dogs burning on tires; the blessing

of God is an intangible, a truth spoken
but fleeting, like the sun sucks up dew.

Still the dreams come at night:
the possessed journeys into impossible light

at sea bottom, where among bones and shells
the truth of ancestral angst is rekindled;

nights galloping the unruly land, a horse
bearing the driving lash of the spirit, the drum;

the limping elder with his walking stick;
the half-man, half-insect spinning webs;

the ladder to the earth from the sky
carrying messages as old as creation.

He wakes with the voice of prophecy
washing his body, his seed, his future.

The judgment is simple:
Your righteousness shall not save you, deceiver,

but the stale brittle of your moistureless soul
will flame into a light for the nations.

Thus saith the Lord of hosts.
All in dreams, these intangibles of life.

HIS PRESENCE

The presence of God is like a flame
  melting the wax beneath it,

like the feet of the wind
  pounding the mountains to rubble,

like the flood of water
  flowing down the slopes,

like the white devouring of glaciers
  through the green of river valleys,

like the precise incisions
  of hill rice growers

shaping generations of steps
  on the mountainsides.

This is the presence of the Lord;
  thanks be to God.

ABOUT THE AUTHOR

Kwame Dawes is part of a new generation of Caribbean writers grounded in a tradition which speaks of possibility. He draws upon inspiration as diverse as Derek Walcott, T.S. Eliot, Lorna Goodison, Bob Marley and Peter Tosh.

He was born in Ghana in 1962, moved to Jamaica in 1971 where he remained until 1987. He has also lived in England and Canada. He now lives in America where he is Professor of English at the University of South Carolina at Columbia.

Kwame is an accomplished broadcaster, actor, dramatist and reggae musician. He has published five collections of poetry, *Progeny of Air*, (Peepal Tree Press, 1994), *Resisting the Anomie* (Goose Lane Editions, 1995), *Prophets*, (Peepal Tree Press, 1995), *Requiem* (Peepal Tree Press, 1996) and *Jacko Jacobus* (Peepal Tree, 1996). *Progeny of Air* won the Forward Poetry Prize for the best first collection of 1994.

Kwame is married to Lorna and they have three children, Sena, Kekeli and Akua.

MORE POETRY BY KWAME DAWES

Requiem

In these 'shrines of remembrance' for the millions of victims of transatlantic slavery, Kwame Dawes constructs a sequence which laments, rages, mourns, but also celebrates survival.

In these taut lyric pieces, he achieves what might seem impossible: saying something fresh about a subject which, despite attempts at historical amnesia, will not go away. He does this by avoiding sentimentality, rant or playing to the audience, black or white. By focusing on individual moments, these poems go to the heart of the historical experience and its contemporary reverberations.

Inspired by the award-winning book, *The Middle Passage: White Ships/Black Cargo*, by the American artist, Tom Feeling, these poems draw us back into the pain, cauterise the lingering infection of slavery and offer the oil of healing.

'A remarkably fresh evocation of the Middle Passage, *Requiem* avoids the temptations of cliche and sentimentality which this theme holds for the unwary poet. A worthy complement to Tom Feeling's drawings, Dawes' threnody nevertheless has its own integrity, self-defining and complete. It is a plangent, searing howl, managed with masterful economy and tact, and moving with all the expected gravity of requiem. The collage of moods, impressions, icons and points of view brings the sufferers of the Middle Passage and their inheritors into the dynamic relationship of a timeless present.'

Edward Baugh

ISBN 1900715 07 4
Price £4.99
48 pages

MORE POETRY BY KWAME DAWES

Prophets

As 24-hour television, belching out the swaggering voices of American hellfire preachers, competes with dancehall, slackness and ganja for Jamaican minds, Clarice and Thalbot preach their own conflicting visions.

Clarice has used her gifts to raise herself from the urban Jamaican ghetto. She basks in the adulation of her followers as they look to her for their personal salvation. Thalbot has fallen from comfort and security onto the streets. With his wild, matted hair and nakedness, he is a deranged voice in the wilderness. Whilst Clarice has her blue-eyed Jesus, Thalbot brandishes his blackness in the face of every passer-by. Clarice's visions give her power; Thalbot is at the mercy of every wandering spirit. But when, under cover of darkness, Clarice 'sins' on the beach, Thalbot alone knows of her fall. He sets out to journey, like Jonah, to denounce the prophetess and warn the Ninevite city of its coming doom. An epic struggle begins...

Brag Magazine wrote '*Progeny of Air* reads like the opening communication from a writer of major significance'; *Poetry Review* said 'I look forward to seeing what *else* this man can do.' Here in *Prophets* that promise is delivered. *Prophets* is an epic poem of vast energy and pace, multi-layered richness and allusive wit. In *Prophets*, Kwame Dawes has written a humane comedy of spiritual striving which will surely be recognised as one of the major works of the decade.

ISBN 0948833 85 8
Price £6.95
160 pages

MORE POETRY BY KWAME DAWES

Progeny of Air

Progeny of Air won the prize for the best first collection in the Forward Poetry Prize, one of the UK's most prestigious poetry competitions. The following is an extract from an article by Linda France in *Poetry Review*:

'*Progeny of Air* takes its title from a single poem describing a fishing trip, referring to the life cycle of the salmon, both actual and hypothetical. this also neatly reflects the themes and concerns of the collection: movement and the impulse of natural energy; the need to go back and revisit meaningful times and places in one's life; a way of living an authentic life, the possibility of growth and self-awareness. The leap and dash of the salmon is also caught in the musical rhythms and striking language.

I am grateful to Kwame Dawes for writing this book and bringing some heat to a grey and chilly autumn. Peepal Tree are bringing out two further books, I look forward to seeing what *else* this man can do.'

'*Progeny of Air* reads like the opening communication from a writer of major significance'

Brag Magazine

ISBN 0948833 68 8
Price £6.95
160 pages